To my Friend Janice

"Be Blessed"

Hey!

LET'S CELEBRATE YOU.

Who, Me?

YES, YOU

We Must Kick Out Discouragement the Dream Killer

MARY-LINDA STEED

Mary-Linda Steed

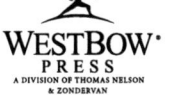

WESTBOW PRESS
A DIVISION OF THOMAS NELSON & ZONDERVAN

Copyright © 2014 Mary-Linda Steed.

All rights reserved. No part of this book may be used or reproduced by any means, graphic, electronic, or mechanical, including photocopying, recording, taping or by any information storage retrieval system without the written permission of the publisher except in the case of brief quotations embodied in critical articles and reviews.

WestBow Press books may be ordered through booksellers or by contacting:

WestBow Press
A Division of Thomas Nelson & Zondervan
1663 Liberty Drive
Bloomington, IN 47403
www.westbowpress.com
1 (866) 928-1240

Because of the dynamic nature of the Internet, any web addresses or links contained in this book may have changed since publication and may no longer be valid. The views expressed in this work are solely those of the author and do not necessarily reflect the views of the publisher, and the publisher hereby disclaims any responsibility for them.

Any people depicted in stock imagery provided by Thinkstock are models, and such images are being used for illustrative purposes only.
Certain stock imagery © Thinkstock.

ISBN: 978-1-4908-3514-3 (sc)
ISBN: 978-1-4908-3515-0 (e)

Library of Congress Control Number: 2014907452

Printed in the United States of America.

WestBow Press rev. date: 05/02/2014

I dedicate this book first to my Lord and Savior Jesus Christ, who literally saved my life. To my mother and father Jessie and Glover Riddick, my husband Willie Steed Jr. To my awesome children Tanya Upchurch, Calvin Purnell Jr. Alexis Moore, my awesome son in law Kenya Upchurch. My wonderful daughter in law Kristy Purnell, and my awesome son in law Tommie Moore Sr. My beautiful grandchildren Christopher Purnell, Harmony Upchurch, Skylar Purnell, Trey Purnell, Brooklynne Dorch, Shayla Moore, Tommie Moore Jr., Aliyah Moore… To my grandfather Robert Ramsey who started teaching us as babies about Jesus. To my spiritual parents Pastors Harold and Alyce Faye Benjamin who taught me the Word of God. It was under their ministry that I accepted Jesus as my personal savior, and grew up with a firm and solid foundation in the things of God. To my present Pastors Ray and Tracey Barnard who are great examples to us and demonstrate how to use our faith and believe God for anything. To my loving and supportive sisters and brother Velma Thomas, Glover Riddick III, Barbara Berry and my cousins Cynthia Mills-Walker and Kimberly Broady. They have been my biggest cheerleaders, supporting me through this whole process. I am truly grateful. My cousins Vera and Yvonne Haines and my cousin Carrie Costner have become Rocks in our family. They will never know how much I appreciate them. I want to say it now. I honor everyone I have mentioned and pray God's blessings on them beyond measure for all they have given me in this life. One more person who God used to mold and shape my character early in life Calvin Purnell Sr. God bless you, Calvin. I want to honor my husband Willie Steed Jr., last but not least. He was the driving force for me writing this book. It was through him I rededicated my life back to Jesus. I learned things about God and myself that I never knew. I grew and developed in ways, I never dreamed. God bless you beyond measure my dear husband. Thank you Holy Spirit for guiding me through this whole process

CONTENTS

Introduction ix

Chapter 1: Discouragement The Dream Killer 1
Chapter 2: Kicking Out Discouragement 7
Chapter 3: Leaning Not on Your Own
 Understanding 13
Chapter 4: He Shall Direct Our Paths 21
Chapter 5: To Be All God Intended You to Be 23
Chapter 6: Learning How to Encourage Yourself 27
Chapter 7: Accepting Who You Are 33
Chapter 8: Loving and Celebrating Yourself 41
Chapter 9: Being on Assignment 49
Chapter 10: The Virtuous Woman 63

INTRODUCTION

"Let's celebrate you". I say it because God wants you to realize how special you are. You are special to God even though you may feel like you're not special to anyone. You are special to God and important to His plan for this earth. Yes, for this earth. You were created to fulfill a special plan that God already preplanned before you were even born. Just as David ran into his destiny, killed Goliath, and saved his people, you, too, can boldly run into your destiny. David had a relationship with God before he killed Goliath. It was because of his relationship with God that he was prepared to do what had to be done, and he was victorious. The same principle applies to us today. Your relationship with God will prepare you as well for what is to come. God will speak to you. He will instruct you on how to kill the lion and the bear so that you will be prepared for your special assignment. When that time comes, you will be ready to do whatever it is God has called you to do without doubt and fear.

You must celebrate you—not in a cocky way but in a way that glorifies God. God is glorified when we walk in His confidence and His strength, and His grace is upon you, which empowers you to succeed in all you were called to do. I remember growing up and not liking myself. I was always putting myself down. I felt worthless and like everyone was better than me, but God poured out His love upon me in such a way that I knew I was loved. Knowing that love, has changed my life. It made me appreciate who God made me to be and not to be intimidated by anyone. I am just as good as anyone. My purpose in God's plan is just as important as David's was when he killed Goliath and as important as Moses' when he lead the children out of Israel and even as the father of many nations, Abraham's. I am a friend of God too.

The Lord says these are the days of special assignments given by the Holy Spirit. You'll be on a mission from God.

You must accept who you are and how God made you. The Spirit of the Lord says to accept yourself and celebrate who you are, not who you hope to be but who you are right now. Hope is for the future, and I'm talking about *right now!* God wants you to walk in confidence, His confidence. It isn't the same as self-confidence because you are not depending on yourself. You are depending upon God, who doesn't fail, the greater one who lives on the inside of you.

I heard Joyce Meyer say, on television, "God, has a unique one of a kind plan for you. A plan that was designed, special for you." God created you unique. Joyce Meyer hated her own voice. She felt it was too deep and sounded like a man. Now her voice is recognized by millions all around the world. God created you an original. You don't have to live and die as a copy. Celebrate your own individuality.

Consider the woman at the well (John 4:1–42). She was a woman whose confidence was in pursuit of always being with a man. She had to have a man. But because of this need, it was driving her life. What is driving your life? Jesus revealed Himself to her and changed her life from that moment on. God has always wanted to be your main focus, your first love, the one you can depend on, the one you can trust with your heart and life. He wants to be the one. So ask yourself, "What is the force driving me?" God will give you the ability to set *realistic* goals for yourself and then help you achieve them. Envisioning yourself improved upon might be new to you; however, it's all part of God's plan, and there is nothing wrong with that. In the meantime, celebrate your originality and find your individuality. What does that mean? *That* can be your feelings, your opinions, your story, your issues on any particular subject that is important to you.

Now is the time for the eyes of your understanding to be opened. Take a good long look at yourself and see yourself as that great person. We are fearfully and wonderfully made in His image. His workmanship created us to love and be loved. Start to see yourself through the eyes of God, who created you. Don't look at your imperfections, your weaknesses, and all those flaws that you see. Take your last look at that person and refuse to think about that anymore. Let's celebrate you! Celebrate your originality because you are the apple of His eye. Remember you are the one that He laid His life down for.

Now I live celebrating who I am and who God made me to be in Christ Jesus here on this earth. I celebrate you, and I'm no longer jealous or envious, intimidated or isolated. I love you for your originality. I finally realized that we are all special to our heavenly Father. When you finish this book, I know you will feel like celebrating your life. It can be so wonderful. Pass on your wisdom and bless another with it. *We* can change the atmosphere because we are the carriers of the Holy Spirit, and like Bill Winston says, "We don't come to take sides. We come to take over." Now begins the journey.

CHAPTER 1

Discouragement The Dream Killer

I will trust in the Lord with all of my heart. I will not lean on my own understanding; however, in all my ways I will acknowledge Him, and He shall direct my paths. I will not be wise in my own eyes. I will fear the Lord and depart from evil.

Discouragement must be dealt with in the spirit. Discouragement is a tool that Satan uses to stop you, to bring you down, to wipe you out, and ultimately to destroy you. He begins to work his plan. First he starts with the mind, feeding you all his lies about your situation and how you are never going to make it. Even if you do, he says, your good life is so far in the future you might as well not even count on it. Fear begins to grip you so that you are paralyzed and begin to say to yourself, "God can't be for me. Look at my situation. Nothing is going right. I will never be able to get out of this. The whole world says I'm nothing, and I'll never be anything, so it must be true. I'm afraid I'll be rejected. I feel like I'm going to perish." Discouragement sets in and deprives you of confidence and hope in order to deter you and to hinder you. Darkness overshadows you so that you can't see the light, you can't see any hope, and everything seems hopeless.

Discouragement is a tool used by the Devil not just to hold you back but to destroy your dreams. Discouragement must be dealt with. As I look into the mirror, who is the man that I see? If I look through the eyes of discouragement, I won't bother to look up because I won't want to see me. I have no confidence it's gone. My loving Father, won't let me continue to feel this way. He truly is the lifter of my head. God wants you confident. God wants you strong. God wants you encouraged and not only encouraged but to be an encourager. We are going to expose Satan's most successful tool, which has caused many to commit suicide, caused many marriages to dissolve, and caused many to miss out on the destiny God intended for them.

When discouraged, you have allowed the plots and schemes of Satan to overtake you. I know you might say, allowed it? It might sound a little coldhearted, but the reality is just that. It was allowed. Allowing it can be done without you even realizing it. The word, *allow* means that you permit it, you acknowledge it, and you grant it. You give it permission to come in. You acknowledge it with all of your emotions. You grant its right to be there, and

Hey! Let's Celebrate You. Who, Me? Yes, You

you give it power as long as you allow it to stay. I'm still talking about discouragement, Satan's tool. He's such a deceiver that you have allowed, and you don't even realize it. Satan wants you to make decisions and choices when you are in a state of discouragement so that he will affect your future.

Discouragement can be a dream killer. If allowed to continue, the dreams and hopes you had for your future can be let go. We all have dreams and hopes of what we want for our futures. It keeps us moving forward, and dreams help us get a vision of the possibilities of our hearts' desires. When I became a believer, a child of God, He immediately began working on me from the inside out. Building me up with His words, comforting me with His Spirit, I actually became hopeful. I felt confidence take root in me, and before long I felt good about being *me*. The Bible says with God all things are possible. God lets your dreams soar to the highest heights, and the sky is the limit. When we are limited or feel limited, you cannot be all that God intended for you to be. In the Bible God demonstrated that we could be more than we even dared to dream was possible.

God wants you to know His love in a personal and intimate way. He picked me up, lifted my head, and made me confident. We are going to expose Satan's tools here. Think about this. Adam was the first man to have fellowship with God. After sin Adam became something he was never meant to be—afraid and fearful. He said it himself, "I was afraid." The same principle applies today. The Devil may not approach you but instead use others dear to us whose voices or words we might consider valuable. "I just don't see you doing this or that." "I can't see you there." "I just can't imagine." Before you know it, you'll be saying, "I can't see." Can you imagine constantly being beaten down like that over and over again? Well, that's how it works sometimes. The Devil relies solely upon what you don't know. What you don't know can kill you.

We all believe ourselves to be fairly intelligent people, imparted with a measure of wisdom for our age, but ignorance says if you aren't educated or taught about certain things, then these negative forces can and will enter your life and rule you. It can be quite horrific. Because of this ignorance, you have permitted or allowed this evil to enter. Knowledge gives you the power to choose. Without it, we will surely perish. Usually we make bad decisions because of what we don't know, but for those of us who are educated, who are taught in the Word of God, and who still choose badly ... well, that's another book. Without recognizing what's going on, discouragement can systematically kill most if not all of your dreams.

There are situations we find ourselves in that are toxic to us—toxic because they are poisoning our system with stress. Stress is toxic to our bodies. God had given us an inward signal that lets us know what is not right

Hey! Let's Celebrate You. Who, Me? Yes, You

for us. Everyone is different, and we must understand that because what bothers me may not bother you. We have become a generation of people who live with and tolerate stress in our lives on a continuous basis. We have suppressed it down, and it continues to compound and compound on top of each occurrence until we get to our breaking points. All along our bodies are being affected by these continual toxic situations, and the breaking points come. It may come in the form of a nervous breakdown or a serious burnout or even worse, a heart attack or stroke. You don't want to go there, but you must do a turnaround and make positive decisions for change in our lives. God is waiting for us to call on Him for help.

Even after being born again, the attacks are still going to come. All of his weapons are no match against what you and I now have. We live in Him, abide with Him, and have access to the secret places. One day on my job I was written up and suspended by my supervisor and director of nurses. This was devastating to me because I have always given 110 percent of my best. I'm always trying to be the best nurse, working through my own pains and personal problems, coming to work when I should've stayed home in bed, and always smiling when I felt like screaming inside. Little by little I was beaten down until discouragement told me how to feel. I felt unappreciated and told myself that I was never going back to that place. At that time I didn't see how the Devil was using this to destroy my future there.

Everything appears hopeless, and then the three D's move in—defeat, despair, and death. Negative thinking takes over. We live in a world where a great percentage of the people are experiencing one or more of the three D's. We live in a world and society of defeat, despair, and death. With the loss of jobs and the inability to get jobs, we see people filled with defeat and despair, feeling like they're going to die. So many hardworking people are losing their jobs and losing their homes. Their stability is falling apart, and they're losing everything that kept their lives secure. Defeat, despair, and death set in. God is our true source of security, not our jobs, not our homes. He is our provider, we must look to Him to meet our every need and he will, by faith. We must learn how to use our faith. There is nothing too hard for our God.

CHAPTER 2

Kicking Out Discouragement

Discouragement has to be kicked out literally because it is a destroyer. If you allow it to stay for even a short period, it can do a lot of damage. We as human beings can be so vulnerable at times. We have different times in our lives that affect our emotions. We are very emotional beings. The emotional part of our beings is a driving force because it's the area of choice. We make choices based on our emotional states. Our soul is made up of our mind, our will, and our emotions. Those three areas are vital for our life choices. You choose what makes or breaks you. Encouragement can make you, and discouragement can break you. The choice is yours. You choose. When discouragement is present, it says, "I don't know about you. I just don't care." Sometimes it takes more than what you have inside of you to pull you out of this mood. For me it took God intervening to keep me from killing myself.

Mary-Linda Steed

I was suicidal starting at the age of nine. As a child, I saw nothing good about life. Life for me was a rough place, and death seemed like the better option. Death to a person with suicidal tendencies will always seem like the best option. I know now that life is worth living, but at those times I couldn't see the other side. If you look at street people, you might say to yourself, "How did they get there? What do they think and how do they feel about the choices that brought them to this place?" I believe it starts in how we think. I heard a minister say once, "You have stinkin' thinkin'." Your stinkin' thinkin' affects your feelings. How you feel affects the choices that you make. If you feel that you are worthless, you will begin to see yourself as worthless. When you see yourself as worthless, you will begin to unconsciously sabotage your life. You will walk away from life. You will walk away from living. You will choose to disconnect from living in every sense of the word. Satan loves this kind of environment. He thrives in this type of atmosphere. It's dark. It stinks. It begins to isolate you, and before you know it, you will be disconnected from reality. I had this opportunity to disconnect from reality, but God gave me a choice. The choice was this: "If you choose to disconnect from reality, you will be on your own. If you choose Me, I will keep your mind in perfect peace." He spoke to me and said, "You don't have to keep your mind. I will keep it."

Hey! Let's Celebrate You. Who, Me? Yes, You

The very thought of me being out there on my own without God scared me. God was a big part of my life, but I was still a very depressed person. I didn't know I was depressed, or I didn't have knowledge about depression. The Bible says, "My people are destroyed for a lack of knowledge." I say this all of the time: "What you don't know can kill you." I would be dead today if God didn't intervene on the suicidal plot on my life. I will never forget that. I was sitting in the bathroom, plotting my suicide and how I was going to do this. I didn't want it to be painful, so I planned to use Valium and alcohol to overdose. Thinking on it now, I may not have even been successful. God spoke to me in that moment and said, "Do you think this life is hell?"

I said yes.

He said, "If you do this, you will be going into real hell, and it's forever."

God told me that if I did this terrible thing, I would enter into real hell and be separated from Him forever. He told me that this life was not hell at all and that I had no idea of what hell really was. It was not created for my soul but for the Devil and his fallen angels. He said the torment I think I know was nothing to compare to what was there, and it would go on forever without end. I was about to end a beautiful gift and begin an eternal nightmare without my God and Father. I realized that this possibility was more devastating than I thought my life was and all because I was listening to the Enemy and not my God. He told me that He has promises for my life He was waiting to fulfill and that He only wanted me to choose life and believe Him. Then I said yes to Him, yes to His grace, His mercy, and His forgiveness. It was like waking up from a bad dream, and everything was changed. My life felt new to me. I commanded depression and every other lying spirit to leave me. I never felt so free. Life became a good thing, and I wanted to live. For the first time in my life I was celebrating, and it was wonderful. I was celebrating God and being His child. I was celebrating being me.

God has empowered us to speak to anything that tries to exalt itself against His Word. He gave me boldness and the confidence to believe it is done. I knew there would be challenges. The unknown can be scary when you don't have faith and courage. God told me to remember that He didn't give me a spirit of fear but one of power and a sound mind. I began to learn about the promises God made to me, and I wanted to have them over my life, not the dark clouds that rained gloom and doom. It felt so good being without depression and fear. You must deal with discouragement by casting it out in the name of Jesus. Bind it and cast it low. Embrace the promises of God over your life and land. Use the power of your tongue to decree and declare that it's done in the name of Jesus. Then you are in agreement with Jesus Christ when He said, "It is finished."

Please don't be confused about this because faith is always tried and tested. Just stand on God's Word, and you will never lose. You might have some hard and trying times but always believe what God has said and do it. That's how we do it, and that's why we always win. With your opened eyes blinded no more, you can see and live His plan and purpose for your life. Jeremiah 29:11 says that God has a good plan for our lives, a plan for good and not evil, one to bring us to an expected end. His love is so completely wonderful. There is so much He wants to show us, so much that He wants us to have here on this earth right now. But first let's delight ourselves in Him. Let God direct your steps and position you to receive the blessing. Watch Him expand you in every imaginable way. Then hold on because the unimaginable is just ahead, and in that place you will be truly overtaken and overflowing with His essence. You will be blessed beyond measure.

CHAPTER 3

Leaning Not on Your Own Understanding

When I cried out to God, "Help, Lord," I knew I must lean on Him to help me. "I don't know what to do because I've been depending on my own understanding, trying to fix things myself, and it's not working." I believe our problems have come to us because we don't always look to God for wisdom but depend on our own understanding. We need our Lord's help every step of the way, and we are trained to figure things out for ourselves. Plus, our lives are very complicated. There are times when we don't know what to do, but we try to figure it out. God wants us to be dependent on Him. He wants us to ask Him for His help, but most of the time we don't.

When I call out to God, "Help me, Lord," I know that I *must* put all my trust and faith in Him to help me. I have tried to work things out for myself, and leaning to my own understanding. Problems arise, we can't handle, we need our God. We don't have to understand everything. We just have to trust and believe God through everything. This is the answer to being free, knowing that we can't but that He can and will. Problems become headaches when our imagined understanding tells us that we don't need our God and Father. But God wants us dependent on Him. He wants us to ask because it will please us to give to someone we love. Same thing applies with our children. Through our eyes, our lives seem so complicated, so perplexed, and many times we don't know what to do, so we try to figure it out until we become so frustrated that we make it worse than before. Being dependent on God means that we don't have to worry or fear. It means that we can count it all as joy because our Father is in control. He has made us promises, and He will bring them all to pass if we just trust in Him. He will bring us to an *expected end* because all things will work together for good for those who love the Lord. So we don't have to trip over every circumstance that comes up. It's just another opportunity for our God to show Himself as mightier than our problems—all because He loves us so much that we can celebrate.

Years ago I found myself in a tight situation. My car had broken down, and I needed it to get to work. At that time I had no money to get it fixed. Suddenly I felt panicky. I didn't know what to do. I thought about not

Hey! Let's Celebrate You. Who, Me? Yes, You

being able to get to work or anywhere for that matter. It was like being paralyzed. I became seized by fear and dread. It had become emotionally draining. My husband was driving my car when it broke down. He called and said he would pick me up in his mother's car. I sat in a chair near the time clock to wait for my husband. I felt exhausted, and I remember sighing and feeling so sad. As I sat back in the chair, I asked the Lord to please help me. I felt helpless. As I positioned myself in the chair, I felt like something was happening around me because I didn't know if I was daydreaming or in a trance.

I seemed to fall backward onto this big white mattress, and all of a sudden the mattress rose up and began to float into the sky like some magic carpet. As I lay there experiencing this elevation and the clouds around me, I felt completely carefree. I raised my arms up to hug them when I heard a peaceful voice ask me, "What are you doing?"

I was so at peace and content that I answered back, "Absolutely nothing." I was in a state of euphoria without a care in the world, and I will never be able to describe the peace I felt.

Then I heard the voice speak again. "That's exactly what you're going to do—absolutely nothing." A short time later my husband came to get me, and we agreed on making a stop before taking his mother's car back. I took all of my papers from the glove compartment, and we went to her house. Upon arriving there, those same feelings came back to disturb me again, and I started to worry about how I would get to work that weekend. I didn't even know how to catch public transportation to get there.

That's when my mother-in-law said, "Just take my car for the weekend." It was music to my ears, and I had done absolutely nothing. God had made a way, and He wasn't finished yet.

That Monday was my day off, and the same negative feelings were there waiting to start in on me. *How can you get your car fixed without any money?* I thought over and over and over. Then the garage called to inform me that the mechanic couldn't start on my car until Wednesday. As I sat at home, I decided to go through my shoulder bag and clean it out. There were lots of papers from my car, and I needed to read everything before I threw anything away. I found some paperwork that looked like a warranty on my car. I called my husband about it. We discovered that the warranty covered all cost to repair my car, and when my car was fixed, the money was there. Praise God. Trusting God is really the only way to go. He takes care of all our needs if we just let Him. He did it all for me, and I did absolutely nothing. There would be many other situations to follow, but I *always won* in the end because of His faithfulness to His Word and me. I pray for ever-increasing faith and trust in God, whom I love.

When God says to lean not on your own understanding, I believe the key to living this out is found in the first part of Proverbs 3:5, "Trust in the Lord with all thy heart." Trusting in the Lord is learned behavior. As I've said earlier, we must be taught, and we must choose to believe. Science has proved that we aren't using our whole brain yet, so we can hardly expect to comprehend the things that are mysteries to us. Therefore, we should be willing to trust God to deposit into us what we can comprehend and prepare ourselves for what is to come. If we learn from our spirit, then we can live in absolute trust and faith in God. This process takes time, and God created time for us. When we trust in the Lord and not our own understanding, we become a threat to Satan and his kingdom of darkness. When he can find no darkness within you, his tempting becomes useless. Jesus showed us how to be victorious over every situation when He said, "It is not my will but my Father's, not my words but my Father's, not my power, but His." Imitating Jesus is doing the will of the Father.

God is in control at all times, and yet some of us think we can have a problem that He can't handle. These are thoughts from undeveloped minds, people who have not yet experienced God and can't believe right now. This is why we pray for them so that they may someday see and know the truth about our creation, what it means to be in Christ, and the eternal benefit of salvation. Satan doesn't want us to trust God. He wants us to believe his lies. Leaning on your own understanding blinds us to what God can do and causes us to think that He failed us. That's just what the Enemy wants. God can never fail, and in Christ we won't either.

You see, His plan for our lives is higher than our own, and that's why He doesn't want us to worry about it. Trusting in the Lord with all our heart removes worry and fear from it. This is how we protect our hearts with the Word of God. The Bible tells us that one who waits (or trusts) in the Lord is never put to shame. These words are life to us. They fill us with hope and deepen our faith to trust in God and not ourselves. Everything we could possibly need in this life and world has already been provided for us through Jesus Christ, our Lord. So we don't have to understand everything. We might not understand why, but we will always win if we faint not. Jesus said His yoke was easy and His burden is light. He knew Father God was watching over His Word to perform it. Everything He said was going to happen. Whatever He says about our lives will happen. This makes me happy and full of joy. I hope you are getting with it too. Life is a celebration of love between the Creator and His beloved creation. Heaven is a place of celebration. Earth can be too.

Our God is a loving Father, a caring compassionate parent whose heart embraces all of us. He has planned our help since our beginning and has provided for all

Hey! Let's Celebrate You. Who, Me? Yes, You

who call upon Him, whatever the need may be. I choose this day and forever to let Him bless my life with His love, His grace, and His mercy. I have suffered through ignorance long enough. I've fouled up so many times by trying to be the mastermind but only being fooled in the end. I finally realized that if I let God be the God of my life and choose to trust Him, He would never let me down. He has ways of helping us that we know nothing about, but when we submit by faith, we'll see some supernatural occurrences and know His mighty hands are working on our behalf. God's way is always right. God's way is always good and better than anything we could ever dream of. God has a track record with me from my beginning. When my eyes were finally opened, I watched Him bring me from blessing to blessing. My cup runneth over, and I am truly overtaken by Him.

A song writer said, "When I looked back over my life and I think things over, I can truly say that I've been blessed. I have a testimony." As a child of God, I know I can depend upon my heavenly Father to help me every step of the way. I can walk in courage and confidence when I'm not leaning on myself because I can fail and God can't. I am no longer under the burden of doing everything right, free from the guilt and pressures of failure and unafraid to meet my future because I don't have to worry about it. That's real freedom. We are blessed to have people in our lives, who would do whatever they could to help us, but unfortunately they are limited in ability. Turn to God first. He is limitless in ability and resources. He will never tire of us. We can't exhaust or deplete Him. It is so good to know that whatever we ask Him in faith and Jesus' name, we will have that thing whatsoever. We have a God-given right to celebrate ourselves because we're not perfect but loved beyond imagination and perfected in Jesus Christ, who paid the price.

CHAPTER 4

He Shall Direct Our Paths

As a child of God, He is directing our paths in life. He has a destiny already mapped out for our lives. Through the ministry of the Holy Spirit, God is constantly speaking to us in that still, small voice, and when we hear and obey, we can never go wrong. The Holy Spirit is constantly on the job, being our helper, leading us and guiding us in all truth. We must make the quality decision of choosing to listen and obey Him. He's been with us from the beginning through every good and bad choice we have ever made. I'll never forget when I was fourteen years old, and I received Jesus as my Savior. Before Jesus came into my life, I was a habitual thief. I loved going into stores, stealing things, and getting away with it. After being born again for about a week, my mind was not yet renewed to the Word of God, and so when I went into a store, I stole this ring I wanted. I left that store with the ring without being caught, but

• 21 •

about a half block away the Holy Spirit spoke to me in that small voice.

To me it was so loud that I thought others could hear it. I was with my sister and my cousin, but they hadn't heard it only I did. He said to me, "You can't do this anymore." Those words went past my head and straight to my spirit, and I knew it was true. I couldn't do this anymore. My spirit had embraced that truth, and I stopped in my tracks and told my sister and cousin what God had said to me. I felt bad about what I had done, and I wanted to take it back; however, I was scared to. What if I was locked up? I decided that I would save up the cost of the ring. Then I'll take the money to the store and leave it on the counter and walk out. That's exactly what I did too. I couldn't seem to rest until it was done. Oh yes, I did ask God to forgive me for stealing. I listened to the Holy Spirit and let Him guide me in what was right for me and what was wrong. The Word of God says that He is my helper, and this is what He was sent to do—to teach and guide me to all truth. And today He is still doing it, and today I'm still listening. I remember an emotion I couldn't define, but I can tell you now because it's still here. Only now it's much stronger. It was *joy*.

CHAPTER 5

To Be All God Intended You to Be

I was a person who never felt that anyone loved me. Even after I was born again, my need to be loved was off the charts. I knew that Jesus loved me, but I didn't *know* it. We can search for love in all the wrong places, and it wasn't until I really developed a relationship with Jesus that I began to feel loved. We've learned misconceptions about love from TV, and we have based our lives on what we saw acted out on the screen. If what I was experiencing in my life didn't measure up to what I saw on TV, then I wasn't getting the love I needed. I had a false idea of what love was all about. My life was built around what I saw on television. I wanted that kind of love, that kind of life and TV husband. I emulated and fashioned my life around fictitious characters. I thought Mary Tyler Moore from the *Dick Van Dyke Show* was the perfect wife and mother. I tried to look like her, dress like her, and act like she did with her make-believe

• 23 •

husband. I fashioned my life around their TV lives. In my real life, however, things weren't acting out according to the TV script, and I was left feeling like a failure because my life didn't measure up to what I perceived love to be. Many of us were deceived from TV stars and their fantasy shows about life.

When I became twenty-five years old, I finally woke up and saw life as it really was and knew that I had to see life for how it really was. I realized that I wasted time when I was in school because I had no direction and I lacked knowledge. The Bible says that people are destroyed for a lack of knowledge. A lack of knowledge and a lack of vision are terrible things. We as teachers of the gospel have a great responsibility to give knowledge of God's Word to everyone we come in contact with. God's Word gives us revelation knowledge on life and what life is all about. We received our knowledge about life from television when I was growing up. Our lives were centered around television sets. That's all we knew! It influenced every aspect of our lives. It shaped our thinking, likes, and dislikes. Television influenced what we wanted to be when we grew up and how we should raise our children. Okay, now that I understand what shaped my thinking, as an adult and a born-again Christian, my thinking has been shaped and developed in many areas. As life has slapped me around as a born-again believer, God's Word has shaped and developed my thinking. If I had paid more attention to God's Word

Hey! Let's Celebrate You. Who, Me? Yes, You

as the manual for teaching me about life, I would have had fewer depressed days and fewer slaps from life.

As long as we are on this earth, we will continue to develop in the will of God. No one on this planet will ever know it all. So the process will continue until Jesus comes back for us. When we learn to sit at the feet of the master, the Holy Spirit, eager like tender young handmaidens totally in love with Him and willing, then He will guide us and show us ourselves as we once were and really are now in Christ forevermore. Beloved, it's still a process. You can't skip over A and B to get to C. What you might miss along the way could be vitally important to your growth and being. But right where you are with every step you take, rejoice in God and celebrate you. If you want to be all that God intended you to be, then you must start right where you are *right now.*

Every move starts from a place. Understand this truth. We are positioned to rise, not fall down, and if we should fall, His hand is always there to help us rise again. We as believers must make it our business to find out what God wants of us and for us. I believe the first step is admitting we don't know what to do. God loves it when we call on Him, when we realize we can't go it alone and need Him. We were not created to be independent of God but to lovingly seek after Him, acknowledging Him in all our ways of service for the kingdom, and to admit that we love and need Him. (Life here on earth with Satan and his crew is proof of that.) Once we've come to really see the light, life here can be better than merely good. Hold on to this now. We are kingdom citizens. This Earth is not our real home. We are on a journey of enlightenment to make Lord Jesus our Savior and to be joint heirs with Him in God's kingdom, to rule and reign with Him as well, and it goes on forever. This is what our true lives are all about. This is why life is worth celebrating no matter what we have to go through. We won't go through life alone, and our end is better than our beginning. Go to God and ask of Him, and the Holy Spirit will tell you all that you can handle at this time, so put that in your heart and celebrate it. To be all that God intended you to be means that you are ready for eternity with Him because that's about how long it will take before you can realize just a small portion of His wonderful love for us.

CHAPTER 6

Learning How to Encourage Yourself

I grew up a depressed child at the age of nine years old, and I wanted to kill myself. My home was a poor one because even though my dad had a well-paying job, he never brought the money home. He was an alcoholic and a gambler, so on payday that's where his money went until it was all gone. We didn't have food in our refrigerator. There were times when our electricity was shut off and we used candles to see, and times when we went without gas to cook the little food we did have. Life wasn't always good for us growing up. My mother cleaned other people's homes to get a few dollars to buy us food. We didn't wear nice clothes or have the plain necessities for life. I experienced stress at a very young age. When I was in elementary school, I would come home for lunch to an empty house. There was no lunch prepared for me. I'd have to go to the store to buy bread and bologna, bring it back home to the empty house, and fix my lunch.

I was afraid of going into an empty house, even my own. I told myself that I would never live this way again, that I would be home for my children and we'd have food, lights, gas, and nice clothes. I didn't know then that these situations were creating strongholds in my life—strongholds of depression and not being loved. My father had those strongholds over his life. He was abandoned by his own father, who was an alcoholic that abused his family. Because my mom had to work and wasn't home for me, I believed she didn't love me. I didn't understand that she had to do this to feed us. If she hadn't worked like she did, then we would have starved. Years later I realized why I felt the way that I did. I didn't know better then, but I sure do now. The day God saved my life, I told depression to be gone in the name of Jesus. I opened my heart to receive the perfect instruction of the Holy Spirit, and He was my guide out of darkness. He taught me how to fill myself with the Word of God. I started rising early in the morning because I was eager to begin my day with God. I could pour out my heart to Him, and He could fill it up with His love and peace. It was good to be alive.

Proverbs 3:5–6 became my anchor. To trust in the Lord with all my heart, lean not on my own understanding, and acknowledge Him in all my ways, I knew He would direct my path. I knew I needed knowledge. His knowledge would become my own, and I would not know destruction. We have to first acknowledge that *He is* and that His words are always true. We need a savior and Jesus is that Savior who came to deliver us from the strongholds of sin. When Jesus took up residence in my life, the darkness was dispelled, and I could see the truth of my life. This can happen for you as well. Ignorance means that you don't know something, but now you do. Now you have someone—someone who loves you so much more than you could have ever imagined. He came and took away everything that could keep you in bondage. He made us alive to God. This means that we are no longer the walking dead but born again in Spirit and equipped with every tool necessary to build new lives in Christ Jesus. We are no longer disconnected from God but one with Him, alive in Him. He now sees us the way that He sees Jesus. Nothing is impossible for us. Now we can walk in His perfect plan for our lives. Behold, all is new, and the former things are passed away. Life without Jesus is no life at all. It means existing in this world but not living in God, who loved us before the world was formed. Being created in His image and having His Spirit on the inside of us means that our words have supernatural power. We have dominion over everything on this earth. The lack of this knowledge can leave one feeling inferior, even though we have His power. Stand up, and recognize that you are everything God says you are. You already possess everything He says you have, and you can do all things through Christ, who strengthens you. Speak the Word of God over yourself and circumstances. You will see yourself and those things change before your very eyes. God has left no stone unturned. He watches over His Word to perform them in our lives. Check this out. We, too, are His Word, and He watches over us to see that we live the way He created us to. Celebrate that when you're feeling down.

The power of life and death is in the tongue. Develop a new language, the words of God. Learn them and see yourself, transformed into the most beautiful of creations, beloved by the Most High, who is powerful beyond human reason. Everything you say has power, and when we speak correctly, we release that power changing everything around us. Be not afraid, dear sisters. The Holy Spirit is here to teach us how to become true masters. He will always guide us in the right direction for our beautiful lives in Christ Jesus. Encourage yourself with this blessed truth. Remember that you are never alone and that even when you stumble and fall as I have, He is always there to take your hand into His and lift you up again. Now at sixty years old I am still growing in this process. I still make mistakes, miss the mark, and beat myself up, but the love of God is so strong in my life that I know I have to keep pressing on. God's chastisement comes with great love. He will never leave or forsake us. Don't be afraid to go through

Hey! Let's Celebrate You. Who, Me? Yes, You

rough times. In the end you always win. We are in the best hands. Nothing can do more for us than He can. Stay encouraged by believing the Word of God.

I am red hot for Him so much so that I scarcely remember the days when I was cold. His love is all-consuming. He's all about life, love, restoration, and peace. Take time out of your busy days and reflect on this wonderful goodness that is all for us. Jesus came to let us know that God is love, and He cares about everything that you are concerned about, and that His plan is always to make our lives better and surely worth living. Celebrating your wonderful life means that you have come to understand there's no beauty anywhere outside of Him, and because you are in Him, you must see your beauty too. It should help to keep you focused when the lies of the Devil speaks to you. Satan is the ugly one now. That was his choice. He was the first fool. He was the first stupid one, the first to fall. Even he didn't know the totality of God. That's why we celebrate because it will take more than all eternity just to learn a little bit more about Him. Celebrate with happiness, joy, and peace that you will be in Him forever. That's what it means to be encouraged, keeping your faith and trust in Him.

CHAPTER 7

Accepting Who You Are

We must accept who we are and how God has made us. Proverbs 31:10 says, "Who can find a virtuous woman? For her price is far above rubies." As far as God is concerned, you are worth more than you can imagine. You are a one-of-a-kind and precious jewel. Our Father sees us this way, and we have to see ourselves the way He does. This isn't always easy when you have been blinded for so long, but just begin to see. God has told us what we are to Him and what we mean to Him, so it's about time we realize it and celebrate it. I don't know about you, but I'm always striving to be the best that I can be. I like dressing nicely. I like my makeup and hair to be perfect to me. When I can pull it together the way I've envisioned, then I feel good about myself, but there are times when I don't pull it together and I don't feel good about myself. Very superficial, right? Yes, I was. Though we may desire to look and feel good about ourselves, our real identities aren't based upon our outward appearance. God had to show me that my thinking was stinking. Proverbs 23:7 says, "As a man thinketh in his heart so is he." Every day I discover how the Word of God renews my mind and changes my thoughts from stinking to pleasing because if I think right, then I'll act right. I used to throw myself the biggest pity parties.

God gave me a vision of what I looked like. It was a vision of a pig wallowing in the mud. (For me it was self-pity.) And I was enjoying it. All of a sudden I became that pig, and I felt its emotion. I actually liked feeling sorry for myself. No matter how many times you get cleaned up from a mess, somehow you can always find you way back to it. Get over yourself. There will always be another you will find more attractive than you, and the only reason she appears so is because you don't see yourself the way God does. It might not happen overnight, but it will happen as soon as you open your heart and see so much wonder and beauty about just being you. God helped me be okay with being me when He saved my life. I had to realize my worth to Him. I had to see myself as valuable. Then I began to see other things about myself that I hadn't known before. Today I always feel good about myself for many reasons, and so will you. The *real you* is beautiful beyond description. *Let her out!*

I had to tell myself that I was a unique woman, that there was no one like me on the face of this earth.

Hey! Let's Celebrate You. Who, Me? Yes, You

God made me an individual with my very own gifts and talents, my own way of expression. Accept who you are and celebrate yourself. We often look at ourselves and are dissatisfied with what we see. For example, I've always had large breasts, but I wanted small ones so that I could walk around without wearing a bra. Women all around the world are paying to have breasts like mine. We're always finding something wrong without noticing everything that is right. We want whatever is fashionable at the time. It's all subject to change. Only God stays the same. Celebrating my individuality is what I do now. I understand that a lot of us grow up around negative views about body images, but as we grow up and mature, we'll learn that this celebration is vital to a healthy life and that there is something inside all of us worth celebrating. You may be someone who has a gift for making people laugh, and you may be a genius at it. Michael Jackson was a genius with his music, and we celebrate him because of it. Every one of us possesses gifts from God, and nowhere else can anyone do it like you. Maybe now your talent remains undiscovered, but when you do find that gift and celebrate yourself in it, the world will celebrate with you.

The Bible tells us that when we receive Jesus as our Savior, the Holy Spirit will come and guide us in all truth. The Holy Spirit taught me how to dress for success in my celebrated life. The most valuable pieces

I own are called the armor of God. It always matches and never clashes with my other clothing. It will be in style as long as we live on earth, and it does a better job of protecting us than our other clothing can. In His armor we can stand against the wiles of the Devil. We can quench his fiery darts. We can crush him under feet and protect our head and hearts all at the same time. God's armor never wears out or fades in the wash. No matter what else you may be wearing, you should never be without the most precious items of your wardrobe.

It's very nice to have pretty clothes, nice shoes, manicured nails, sharp hairstyles, and perfumes; however, if you don't wash your body, it will stink no matter what you have, and all your perfume won't help either. God has strategies for everything we do. He has the kind of plan that never fails. The armor of God is designed to protect and serve us. The helmet of salvation covers our heads, ears, and necks. It stops the Devil from attacking our minds through our ears, and it blocks the deadly works of gossip, which God hates, from the lies the Enemy speaks to stir up negative emotions and cause us to act ungodly. And it doesn't mess up our hairdos. We can even sleep with it on. Wearing the waistband of truth means you won't be caught with your pants down. It holds the truth of the Spirit tight in place around you, and it has compartments that attach to your breastplate.

Your breastplate of righteousness is really how we wear Jesus. Jesus mounts a guard over our hearts because

Hey! Let's Celebrate You. Who, Me? Yes, You

it's where He lives. When we asked Him to come into our hearts and make them new, He did. In the Bible feet and shoes demonstrate how we stand and walk. When we wear the boots of the gospel of peace, we are prepared to crush, stomp, kick, and walk over anything that comes against our peace. It's the best pair of shoes you can wear. The sword of God is His Word. It has a doubled-edged sharpness to pierce and cut down anything in its way, and the shield of faith is full length, which means it stops all the devices of the Devil from getting in. They fall to the ground, and we crush them underfoot and maintain our peace. Our lips look more appealing when we wear praise, prayer, and worship on top of the different colors of lipsticks we wear. Our Father has us covered from head to toe, and one size does fit all. Our personal and intimate relationship with God gives our individuality its own role to play in the kingdom plan for the world. So the next time you feel like you don't count, just remember that you are required to perform a task that only you can do and that you are empowered to see it through. That's why we not only celebrate ourselves but one another. I have something to give you, and you have something to give to me. I can see your light and not lose sight of my own. This is in no way conceited. It is called being the child of God and walking in the benefits of being thus. It's a great life to live in Christ Jesus and to share.

I have to admit that my walk wasn't always easy, but I can say that God was always with me every step of the way. I can't number the many times that I fell, but He never failed to pick me up again. Today I look back on the days and nights of darkness and thank the Lord for deliverance, for the freedom I've lived from just making the right choices. Now as I look upon the blessings of living with Jesus, I find that no good thing was ever held back from me. Jesus said, "All things are possible to him who believes." I am a believer in Him, His love, and His promises. Everything I have believed in Him for has come to pass in my life. My dreams and hopes have been fulfilled. I have my beautiful family, my dream home, and love. I have good health and peace in my life. Truly I am a blessed woman. I still have new dreams and hopes for my future, new goals and visions to achieve. Habakkuk 2 says, "Write the vision and make it plain on tablets, that he may run who reads it for the vision is yet for an appointed time. Earlier in the book I talked about vision and seeing for real. I touched on how discouragement was a dream killer, but now that you know the truth about yourself, you have the power to overcome.

No one can give you a vision. It is on the inside of you. Spending time with God and meditating on His Word will release a vision for your life. It will reveal the real you. It's sad but true that many people still don't know who they are and what is theirs in life, but keep praying for them that their eyes become open to the glorious plan God has for their lives. God's Word says that He will not see you ignorant. That means that we must ask of Him what His plan and purpose for our talents and gifts is. If we ask, He will surely answer. No one needs to walk around aimlessly, struggling in darkness. What God has for you is for *you* and no one else. I can't operate in someone else's gift and talent. I operate and am successful in my own. It's the beauty of you being you and me being me. You are not responsible for my purpose. You didn't make me, but you might just be someone playing a part in my success. God bless you always.

CHAPTER 8

Loving and Celebrating Yourself

Science and medicine have proven that a good attitude about yourself promotes good health and can keep you healthy. Imagine what state of health you could walk in if you really loved yourself. Here's the difference: The world only loves what it considers beautiful and that which it can control. So if you find fault with yourself and nothing to like about yourself, then you have judged yourself like the world does, but when you say, "Hey, I'm not perfect, but I like me anyway." It won't matter to you what other people say. You will beat your own drum. God knows all about you. You're the one who doesn't know. It's up to you to find out about yourself. Let God help you do that. I want you to understand that our uniqueness and individuality inhabit us on the inside, not the outside. On the outside we all look the same—human. Inside is where we differ from everyone else. We can see so much in other people. Why is that?

It's because we haven't yet believed what God says about us, and if you don't like yourself, then you certainly cannot love yourself. That's why it's so important to focus on God first.

When we realize how much God loves us, the first thing we feel is unworthiness. It's true we aren't, but that didn't change a thing about God's love. He still loves us long and strong. Nothing we have done has changed that fact. Now we have eyes to see that if He can love us as we are, then we should be able to love ourselves. Whatever needs work or help in us, God is the fixer. To Him He made us perfect (made in His Image), but He wants us like Him in character as well. The only way we can come to love and celebrate ourselves is to know and understand that God is love and that love is God. When we live in Him and He lives in us, then we're in love. We are one with the most powerful force in and beyond the world. When this takes root in us and we believe it, now we can express it outside ourselves. Now we can tell the Devil, "I may not deserve it, but I'm in love."

Feeling unworthy never stopped the love. Any other force is powerless against it. So even when you feel bad, sad, fat, ugly, and any other negative way about yourself, just remember what the Word says, "Nothing can separate us from the love of God." Get into God's presence, seeking Him to show Himself or His love to you. When you then realize how immeasurably deep or high and vast it is, you can become so filled that it must need outward release or expression. That's the time when you will begin to love yourself. We were created to be with Him forever. He laid down His life to make it so. This kind of love is incomprehensible to the Word. That's how the Devil comes in to deceive us. He knows if he can keep us away from love, we have no power against him. So he preoccupies us with the nonsense of this world. If you were once good at putting yourself down, you should be better at picking yourself up now that you have the truth. Now that you're in love, you will want to take care of yourself better than before. You want to get up, wash up, brush your teeth, smell good, and go before the Lord just because you know how much He loves us. You may give all these considerations to a spouse, kids, friends, and employers, yet they won't tell you that they care about all you do. As humans we need to connect soul to soul. It's nice when we get compliments about ourselves in whatever capacity. It drives us to do more.

Movers and shakers don't throw pity parties. They don't make time for it because they already see themselves as successful. Kingdom heirs don't throw pity parties because we've been delivered from the hand of the Enemy. We celebrate our lives in Christ and one another. Loving yourself is a requirement whether you know it or not. It's the only way you can share God or love with another, and it's the way we get it back from God through people, even those who don't like us very much.

Nothing stops the love. Don't feel bad when you're not appreciated. Sometime you're just not understood.

Because we are unique individuals, we cannot expect others to think, feel, and act as we do. They have a right to be themselves. We become critical when someone disagrees with us. We don't see their individuality. What we see is stubbornness and a failure to get along. The flesh fights for attention. You and I are aware of what it will do to get it. We want to be different, but we want to be like someone else. *Just because you accept yourself doesn't mean that you love yourself.* The Bible says, "We are to love our neighbors as we love ourselves." That's why it's important to educate yourself *about* yourself. When you don't like what you see about yourself, you may go on to imitating people based on your observation of how they look, talk, walk, and possess. We can see the good and bad in others as well as ourselves. The problem is that we don't see ourselves as the same—no better and no worse. The Bible says, "God is no respecter of persons." Unfortunately we are. We judge through ignorance, but God just loves. So why don't we love ourselves?

To accept means to take. We accept many things, some that aren't good for us. When we accept or take from the wrong source, it will have a negative effect on the inside of us and then manifest on the outside, causing chaos. Why would we accept what we don't like or want? Because we are deceived to believe that we have no choice. The Word of God can teach you all

Hey! Let's Celebrate You. Who, Me? Yes, You

about yourself. Your likes and dislikes aren't what make you special. Everyone has those, but it's your walk with God that makes the difference. If you want to imitate someone, then imitate Jesus Christ. Our Lord has said, "If you have seen Him, they you have seen the Father." It's time to accept or take what the Bible says about you and believe it. Then you can take what God has for you and share it with your neighbor. Take it, give it, and celebrate it.

I have grown to appreciate people for who they are. Everyone is important and worthwhile. Don't get me wrong, the Bible does talk about people we should have no dealings with, and it doesn't change their purpose or reason for living. Everyone still has value. If you run across negative people and your light just can't get through, walk in love but also walk away. Just keep it moving. Be in prayer for the lost and the furious. Forgive them of the offense like Jesus did when He said, "Father, forgive them for they know not what they do." When I was really angry at people and felt like I hated them, I'd want God to hate them too because of what had happened to me; however, God loves unconditionally, and He wants the same of us. We can't plot and plan the hurt of others regardless of what's been done to us, and people can do some very terrible things. Vengeance belongs to the Lord, and He will repay. We have a hard enough time trying to walk in love. We don't need to plot out how to hurt someone as well. When you love someone as you do yourself, you just can't hurt that person. Remember love never fails.

Believe me, it's easier to walk away and trust God, whose ways are not like ours. His thoughts are not like ours. That's why we do what He says to do at all times. Then we don't have to wear our emotions on our sleeves. Every year on New Year's Day I get a do-over. I like to make resolutions. I look forward to the day because it gives me another chance to do things better than I did the year before. I see good things come and the useless pass away. I've watched God bring me up from faith to faith and glory to glory. I know that if I didn't love what God loves about me, I could never have come this far in my life or the life of my family and all those whom I love so dearly. Change comes whether we like it or not, but being changed by the Spirit of God is far better than trying to do it by yourself. Doing the same thing and hoping for different results is called insanity. Doing it God's way is called being in love. I want this for you, beloved—to live freely in love, to have everything you need in this life and beyond so that you can remain joyful. If you don't start accepting, loving, and celebrating yourself right now, your joy in the Lord can't grow, and neither will you.

The greatest gift to all of us, is salvation, and we receive it by faith through grace from God. We can be tall, short, skinny, fat, bald, knock-kneed, smelly, etc. You get the point. It really doesn't matter, but you can't bring anyone into the kingdom if you aren't happy about being there yourself. Where is your light, your joy, and your peace? Our real beauty comes from the Spirit within us, and we reflect that beauty to the outside. You can't believe you're beautiful until you *know* that God is, and when you finally get it, your light will start to shine. Begin to speak something good about yourself every day. Meditate on God's Word until your soul grabs hold of it. You will start reflecting what you believe in your life, and when others see that change in you, they might want it for themselves.

Love and celebrate yourself. Be thankful for how God made you. Tell yourself that you are a child of God, beautiful, unique, and one of a kind. There's no one like you. You'd only be speaking the truth, and when you can love others as yourself, you'll make them feel beautiful too. God made you to be a gift in this world—a gift full of blessings. When you give love to people in a pure way, you'll become a precious gem to everyone you touch. Don't tell yourself that you have nothing to give. That's just not true. With your gifts and talents you can change the world. Your joy and happiness is in your giving. The Bible says to "give and it shall be given unto you good measure, pressed down, shaken together and running over will men give unto your bosom." Some might think this speaks only about money, but I believe it embodies whatever you give of yourself.

Mary-Linda Steed

It could be some of your time, food, shelter, or clothes—anything meeting the needs of another, the smallest act of kindness. These little acts of kindness can go a long way in somebody's life. You are blessed to be a blessing. I believe that we were all created to be a blessing in someone's life. Be available for God to use in you whatever way He wants.

CHAPTER 9

Being on Assignment

Sometimes we as parents make the mistake of choosing occupations for our children, never considering what they want at all. A very influential father might say, "I'm a lawyer, and you are going to be one too." Or a compassionate mother might say, "We need a doctor in the family, so you're going to med school." You may not want to be either of those professions, but because you have a need to please, you struggle to become what someone else wants for you. Sometimes it may work out, but most times it doesn't. Sometimes we try to fit a square into a round hole. That's why we adapt to situations or occupations but never really fit in. Parents who are very observant can pick up on the desires of children. Others may guess, and the rest don't care. I was fortunate.

I knew I wanted to be a nurse. I believed that was what I was meant to be. I was gifted in this area.

Mary-Linda Steed

While I was in nursing school, I was so excited about working with children. It's just what I had to do—work in pediatrics. That was the best job for me. However, when I got there, it wasn't the way I had imagined at all. I couldn't stand seeing the children sick. I cried all the time and was completely useless. I couldn't function at all. It was by accident that I started working with geriatric patients and found all my cylinders turning with the same excitement I'd had for the children. There everything came easy to me. I didn't mind the hard work, because I loved the job so much. Now after thirty-five years of working with geriatric residents, I have the honor and pleasure to teach everything I've learned over the years in this field. I'm teaching and preparing people to be CNAs (certified nursing assistants).

I had a desire to teach a Bible study class, and I took the job to sharpen my teaching skills; however, I discovered that I was really good at teaching the nursing class. The most important of all my discoveries was that I needed the guidance of the Holy Spirit to do all I had accomplished. I prayed for Him to show me how to do this and to open my ears and heart to His directions, and He did just that. He was my guide through everything. I celebrate that.

My nursing career changed because of my encounter with a woman I had touched earlier in my career. She was a patient who at that time was deeply depressed. She would sit slumped in her chair with her hair falling all around her face, and she had a urinating problem that she also seemed to care nothing about. I struggled with how to approach her because she didn't seem to want any care from anyone, but I knew that something had to be done for her. Suddenly I felt that she was my assignment from God. He wanted me to touch her life with His love and lift her head, make her smile, and help her rediscover her life. I was willing, but I just didn't know what to do. So knowing that God knows best, I trusted entirely in Him to instruct me. I quietly approached her and took notice of her surroundings.

She had makeup on the windowsill and beautiful nightgowns hanging in her closet. I saw that she had good taste and probably possessed a hidden elegance underneath that depression. I asked her if I could wash her and freshen her up. Her response was, "Why not?" After that I asked her if I could comb her hair and apply her makeup. Her response was, "Why not?" I combed her hair and asked if I could cut her hair and give her straight bangs over her forehead, and she said the same, "Why not?" I did so and pulled her hair back into a ponytail. I began to apply her makeup, and the transformation was astounding.

I stood back and looked at her. She looked like a different woman. I said, "Wow, you look like a movie star." I decided that my supervisors needed to see this, so I went to get them. They felt the same as I did. They told her that she was beautiful too. It seemed to change her attitude. I could tell that she felt better because she was smiling. From that day forward she was no longer slumped over. She was now perked up and happy. She was applying her makeup and dressing herself in those beautiful gowns she had. She was supposed to go into a nursing home, but because of her dramatic change, she was able to go back to her home. She also changed something in me. Just a little bit of care and kindness can really help restore a life, and I knew this job meant more to me than just a paycheck. I had made a difference in someone's life, and that made me feel good about my own. I praised the Lord for confirming my gift. I would never go back to the person I used to be. She was gone forever. This was something to celebrate, and I did. I still do ... right now.

From the moment you are born again in Jesus, the Holy Spirit begins His work on your life. Wherever there is darkness, He will dispel it with His light. His work on me began with raising my self-esteem. Showing me that I was valuable dispelled my feelings of hopelessness. Jesus raised me up with Him until I went from high esteem to God-esteemed. The Devil's power was broken over me. I didn't want to be anyone else. I just wanted to be me and do what God desired for my life. Assignments keep us employed in the kingdom. It doesn't matter what we are called to do. If we'll do it fearlessly with a good attitude and a willingness to please God, then we will reap His willingness to please us. "Delight yourself in the Lord and He will grant the desires of your heart." *Believe it!*

Earlier in the book I shared about how I used to put myself down and called myself defeating names. I helped the Devil keep me down. I didn't know any better, but now free in Christ I know that it's the assignments that release the ability to flow in the gifts. So many things work together in the kingdom and every part of life. Simple acts of kindness and acts of love will activate kingdom power in your life to change not only your life but the world as well. Just like we have angels on assignment, we have work to do too. It's not always easy. The Devil never stops trying to hinder. Just remember that's all he can do, hinder but not stop us. He really has been defeated and we must not forget that. We are the empowered of the Most High, and any assignment we receive from Him, we are *able* to perform. We have everything needed to do it. Take a moment to realize how really wonderful you are because of our Father.

Being a blessing is an assignment. It walks hand in hand with purpose. Everyone wants to know what is, my purpose? Your purpose will be discovered as you spend time in His presence. The real you will unfold right before your eyes. You will begin to see yourself the way you never have before. Now that you have opened eyes, I hope you will see. God made you perfect in every way. Just as He is, so are we. *Get it, take it, believe it, and celebrate.*

Assignments are also challenges. Through them we learn how much we have grown up because God won't give us what we're not ready for. His perfect love casts out *all fear.* So now unafraid, we can boldly go forward, asking "What's next, Lord?" with eagerness, knowing that we won't fail because He can't. This only happens when we are surrendered to God and obedient to Him without question or doubt. Now it's okay to ask questions, but not because you doubt or fear but only when you don't understand. Sometimes there's no time to question but to only do the thing you were assigned to do. You will be blessed for being faithful, trusting, and obedient, and God will be glorified.

Some assignments are designed to take us out of our comfort zones, where we must depend solely upon God. It's a challenge to test our faith in our abilities. We may have gifts and talents, but they need our ability in order to perform them. God gives us the ability. We get if from His Word, which says *we can.* He has already supplied us with every needed thing to do our work. You might not like it but just do it. He always knows best. You may not like the beginning, but you will most assuredly love the end. There will always be negativity in the world, always a dark sided, but it's necessary for us to see ourselves an overcomer, and conquerors of it through the trying of our faith. Welcome the assignments because they bring even more reason to celebrate you and me. Don't you think it's good?

Hey! Let's Celebrate You. Who, Me? Yes, You

This is why we can count it all as joy. Because God has equipped us, victory is ours, and the glory is the Lord's. People who walk in their supernatural power welcome challenges. Even our children love to be challenged. They just naturally love to win. We should be blind only to defeat. When you tire of the Devil and the nonsense that comes with him, suit up and say, "Come on, fool." You'll see those devils run in every direction except toward you. Isn't that worth lifting holy hands in praise for? Through all the good times and the not-so good, God is always with us, always loving on us and wanting to take us to even higher places in Him. Assignments are needed to fulfill God's plan for mankind. Being blessed for kingdom work is such an honor. Embrace yourself today. There's something out there that needs doing, and it can't be done without you.

In the meantime, live, laugh, and always love. Enjoy your life and the lives of others. It's good to appreciate and admire the qualities others can bring to your life. We can adapt some positive ways of other people and make our own lives happier or easier. I might take your suggestion about my concerns, flip it to meet my style, and welcome the change. We can all learn from one another and make good contributions to one another's lives. Sharing ideas has both positive and negative outcomes. Admiring and appreciating and even incorporating different styles have its limitations among people. Sometimes people don't like to see their style with others. We don't like feeling invaded when we don't want to share and when our idea is taken anyway. A good example of this is seen with fashion designers. Most of them design clothing for slim women only and think it's degrading to design for the full-figured woman. Thank God for the designers who are talented enough to do it for all sizes and let everyone look and feel fabulous. It's the same principle in life and business.

That's why we celebrate one another. Be willing to share your gifts and talents. Use what works for you because everything won't. Your next assignment may be to give something away that is very valuable and dear to you. Through giving, we find out just how charitable we really are. An assignment may consist of you sharing an invention with someone who can promote better than you. In order for the world to benefit from it, you must involve other people. We need one another to get it done. The Bible has all the answers about how to do it. It's already mapped out. The only real problems we face are the ones invented by us trying to do something without God, doing a job He didn't assign to us, and making a mess of things. God is always right.

When my assignment was revealed to me, it required that I do something I once thought impossible. I was required to care—not just about myself but for others too. My assignment and destiny is to establish a ministry of care, to help people physically and spiritually, to educate, about the real joy of life, Jesus Christ. Honestly

Hey! Let's Celebrate You. Who, Me? Yes, You

I have run away from many of my assignments because of fear and not understanding that I was equipped to be a success. It wasn't easy for me to see myself doing for others. In my walk with God, He showed me what I needed and then helped me to understand why.

My help ministry began when I discovered I wanted to be a nurse. I was willing to do whatever it took to become a nurse. Then my love for children revealed that I was too emotional to care for them properly. When I ended up working with geriatric patients, I then became aware of my true assignment. Truth is that assignments never end. Our Lord and Savior, was also on assignment. He accepted His assignment from the Father, well aware of what it required Him to do. Praise Him forever. Not one of us will ever have His assignment, and what it did for us was done for all time. It will never be done again. Because of Jesus, we have abundant life forever, not just here on earth. There is no bad assignment. When we are dealing with humans, we have to know that some are suffering through the same things we did in the past, while others are having experiences that we never had to endure. So when we encounter them, we must release the compassion of Jesus to show them that we care. Sometimes just a little smile can make a world of difference to a hurting person.

Think of what the world would be like if we all cared for one another. There would be peace like we never knew before; however, we are not all caring people, and the world isn't that way. That's why we must do all that we can to let the sick and hurting see Jesus in us and gravitate toward Him. Our lives must reflect Him. We are approaching the end of this age, and we don't know how much time we have left. Every minute counts for us as believers to help all. Even when we are rejected, let us continue to care because someone did it for us, and we will continue to rejoice and celebrate because of it. The assignments won't end even after we leave this place.

The Bible describes the Word of God as a mirror. A mirror is used to reflect anything that is in front of it. Every day we look into a mirror to check how we look. A mirror is a necessity for all of us. We would not dare think of leaving home without looking into the mirror. Would you? I wear makeup every day, and I need my mirror to see that I apply it the right way. We use them to see that everything on the outside looks the way we want to. It can only reflect the outer image of us. God's mirror reflects beyond what you see on the outside. His mirror reflects what needs to change on the inside.

Earlier I spoke about us being perfect, and our real selves are perfect, we are spirit. Our spirit is the only part of us that is born again. We possess a soul and we live in a body. Our soul is our mind, our will, our emotions that must be renewed by God's word. We live in a body that is corruptible. It has the ability to destroy its self. This is why God wants us to make that change. Change how you feel about yourself, value

Hey! Let's Celebrate You. Who, Me? Yes, You

yourself. To God you are most valuable. He paid a high price for you. He gave His only begotten son just for you.

We must look into the mirror of God's Word and allow it to change us internally. God wants us to know who we really are, what we have and what we can do in Him. He tells us everything about the earthly life and the supernatural life and gives us the right to choose what we want.

We have yet to understand the power we possess in Jesus. We still don't get it, or even worse, we don't believe it. We can't walk in the authority God has given us. We can't have dominion. We can't speak to mountains in our lives. We can't complete assignments. We can't walk after the spirit when we doubt or don't believe. The Word of God will show you where you're at. Then it's up to you to say, "Lord, I submit to your way of doing things." Not my will but your will be done in my life.

It is the assignment of every believer to be a doer of good. God has made it clear through His Word about how we should treat ourselves as well as others. You might say, "Everybody doesn't deserve good treatment." That is so true, but we've got it anyway through the shed blood of our Lord. None of us deserve what we have been blessed with, but we have it just the same. We are assigned to be doers of the Word and not just hearers. The Bible doesn't say, "Just be nice." It says to be doers of good. It's more than an act. It's a way of life for us, and God said not to get weary in well doing. So we can see that this is a requirement, an assignment.

This is asked of us because of the things that grow in us from doing, such as honesty, integrity, and the greatest, love. When people reject you or are nasty toward you, they're running from the very thing they need the most. This is why we must not be weary. Just when you're about to quit is when *you're needed the most*, and it's our Father who sees that. He is a rewarder of everything we do. Your labor is never forgotten. God is the paymaster, and He will see to it that your harvest is a good one. As we sow, so shall we reap. As long as there is seed, time, and harvest, this shall always be so. Be a doer of good means to be that way under all circumstances. Jesus went about doing good, to all whom He encountered.

It didn't even matter how they treated Him. He just went about doing what He was called to do. We've got to be the same way, imitators of Jesus. He never rejected His assignment, and because He didn't, we have the wonderful benefits of salvation today. I can happily celebrate that, and it encourages me whenever I feel like I can't or don't want to continue and whenever I might find myself becoming weary. The assignment really doesn't require our thoughts about it. We can let our flesh talk us right out of what we need to be doing. That's why we don't lean on our own understanding but trust God in all our ways of service to Him. Doing good, for others puts us in the position of being more like

Hey! Let's Celebrate You. Who, Me? Yes, You

God. His thoughts and ways are not like ours, so when we imitate what we know about Him, our thoughts and ways become more like His. Now that's really *good*.

God is waiting for us to arrive. To develop and mature in spiritual growth (truth and power) so that we can fulfill our purpose on this earth, our destinies. He wants us to accept His Word about ourselves, get it into our hearts, believe it, and be in position to be used in this world for His glory. But we have to learn how to think, speak, and act to show ourselves worthy. The Bible says that as a man thinketh so shall he be. Another translation says, "As a man believeth so shall he be." Thinking is okay, but knowing and believing is far better. Believing and knowing boosts confidence. Thinking indicates that you haven't made a decision. Make one now.

Choose to believe every word of God. Choose to believe what He says about you. Choose to accept and believe. Settle this thing in your heart now so that you can go about your business. *Release your faith now.* It's time to walk in our new birth. We have been given faith to believe God. That faith equips us to succeed, to speak to mountains, to rise to new heights in Christ and fulfill our destiny. Faith is an absolute necessity. We must have it do all the things that seem impossible. It's not a feeling or mental condition. It is the power to bring things to pass in our lives, and without it, we are not pleasing to God. We need faith to believe no matter what things look like around us. It is the substance for things hoped for, not yet seen or manifested in our lives *yet*. When I realized that I possessed something already pleasing to God, I made it my business to find out how to use it. It became my heartfelt intention never to be without it in every area of my life. To this day it has never failed. It feels so deeply exciting to know that I am pleasing to God because I have faith in Him. No matter how busy my schedule is, I always pause to celebrate that I please God and delight myself in Him because He cannot fail. I celebrate God loving me and empowering me to be like Him. When I look in the mirror today, I can really celebrate who God has made me to be. He has molded and shaped me into a more loving, compassionate, and giving person.

CHAPTER 10

The Virtuous Woman

She is in every born again woman, study her, to become her.

Proverbs 31:10   Who can find a virtuous woman? For her price is far above rubies.
(Where is she? She's in me, and I am a priceless gem. I am really valuable.)

Proverbs 31:11   The heart of her husband doth safely trust in her, so that he shall have no need of spoil.
(She is not a waster.)

Proverbs 31:12   She will do him good and not evil all the days of her life.
(She will do him good and not evil all the days of her life.)

Proverbs 31:13   She seeketh wool, and flax, and worketh willingly with her hands.
(She is not a lazy woman.)

Proverbs 31:14   She is like the merchants' ships; she bringeth her food from afar.
(She is a woman of vision with no limits.)

Proverbs 31:15   She riseth also while it is yet night, and giveth meat to her household, and a portion to her maidens.
(She spends time with God to get direction for her day. She has hired help so that her household continues to run smoothly.)

Proverbs 31:16   She considereth a field, and buyeth it: with the fruit of her hands she planteth a vineyard.
(She is a business woman. She is a sower. She sows for her future. She understands seed, time, and harvest.)

Hey! Let's Celebrate You. Who, Me? Yes, You

Proverbs 31:17 She girdeth her loins with strength, and strengtheneth her arms.
(Her emotions are under control. She understands that exercising keeps her body fit, but it also releases the hormone of tranquility. She doesn't have time for stress. Her strength is developed by her relationship with God, using God's Word to strengthen her inner man. "I can do all things through Christ who strengthens me.") She understands strength is built and strength is developed. Spiritually and physically.

Proverbs 31:18 She perceiveth that her merchandise is good: her candle goeth not out by night.
(She knows that she is a good thing. She always makes time to ministers to her husband's needs.)

Proverbs 31:19 She layeth her hands to the spindle, and her hands hold the distaff.
(She is creative and allows her creative juices to flow.)

• 65 •

Proverbs 31:20 She stretcheth out her hand to the poor; yea, she reacheth forth her hands to the needy.
(She gives out to those in need. She is a giver and has a givers heart. She's blessed to be a blessing.)

Proverbs 31:21 She is not afraid of the snow for her household: for all her household are clothed with scarlet.
(She has sowed. She has prepared ahead of time, to make sure her family's needs are met.)

Proverbs 31:22 She maketh herself coverings of tapestry; her clothing is silk and purple.
(She is a stylish woman. She loves to look and dress nice.)

Proverbs 31:23 Her husband is known in the gates, when he sitteth among the elders of the land.
(He looks good because of her. She shows him the highest respect.)

Hey! Let's Celebrate You. Who, Me? Yes, You

Proverbs 31:24 She maketh fine linen, and selleth it; and delivereth girdles unto the merchant.
(She is a business woman, an entrepreneur, and a support to other entrepreneurs.)

Proverbs 31:25 Strength and honour are her clothing; and she shall rejoice in time to come.
(Strength and honor is her character.)

Proverbs 31:26 She openeth her mouth with wisdom; and in her tongue is the law of kindness.
(Her tongue is operating under this law of kindness.)

Proverbs 31:27 She looketh well to the ways of her household, and eateth not the bread of idleness.
(She has no time for gossip and discontent.)

Proverbs 31:28 Her children arise up, and call her blessed; her husband also, and he praiseth her.
(They confess she had empowered us to prosper.)

Proverbs 31:29   Many daughters have done virtuously, but thou excellest them all.

Proverbs 31:30   Favor is deceitful, and beauty is vain: but a woman that feareth the LORD, she shall be praised. (Having God's favor is important to her)

Proverbs 31:31   Give her of the fruit of her hands; and let her own works praise her in the gates.
(She doesn't have to go around bragging about her accomplishments. "I did this. I did that." Her fruit will speak out her praises.)

When I worked at Bryn Mawr Terrace, every year my job would give us an in-service so that we could be first-class employees. They had their conception of what first-class meant to them. I've taken their meaning and made it my own vision of the virtuous woman. I'll share it with you, and you can share it too.

The First Class Virtuous Woman

First impressions are lasting impressions, what you are remembered for. The way you greet, smile, and sincerely offer your assistance to help someone. This

Hey! Let's Celebrate You. Who, Me? Yes, You

is what they will remember, and you may not have a second chance.

C is for commitment........You are committed to who you are, and who you are becoming.
L is for leadership..........You are a leader. You spend time with God getting His direction.
A is for attitude............You have a good attitude, about yourself and others.
S is for service.............You are a woman of service, always willing to serve.
S is for support............You are always willing to do what you can to help and support others.

This is from my heart to yours

You are fearfully and wonderfully made. For as a man thinks in his heart so is he. How do you see yourself? How you see yourself is also how the world will see you. If you don't like what you see, make that change with God's help. You can change yourself for the better. The world is waiting for you. When the real you comes forth, you will celebrate yourself, and the world will celebrate you as well. Celebrating yourself is not having a big head. It is appreciating what God has done and what God has made you to be. It is really celebrating God's masterpiece. God, be glorified through my life an instrument of use. Without Him we are nothing, and with Him we are everything. God took time with you when He created you. You are not an afterthought, and you were not created from happenstance. You were specifically wired for God's purpose and plan, and He knew you would affect this world like no one else could. Your individuality was on purpose for God's specific plan. You can go through life and never know what God has purposed for you. My whole purpose for celebrating you is done so that you will allow God's plan to unfold before you. If you continue to walk around and feel unworthy and worthless, you will not appreciate the uniqueness and discover who you are and why you are here. When you learn to appreciate yourself, God will reveal to you why you are here. That revelation will cause you to appreciate every opportunity you get to do what you were created to do. Think about those who write songs, who write books, and who create masterpiece paintings. I see how those songs, those books, those paintings, make others happy. It makes me see you must bring forth that gift. That is important to the world. God so loved the world that He gave, His Son, and His Son was created to be our life source and bring life into this world. God so loved the world that gave us a purpose

Hey! Let's Celebrate You. Who, Me? Yes, You

intended to bring His life into this world. Each one of us who is recreated in the image of God has the ability to bring life to everyone, and life gives each one of us a reason for living. We should all be about the business of living. Jesus said, "I came that you may have life and have life more abundantly." We should live life to the fullest until it overflows, and life overflowing is a life that gives. You might say, "What do I have to give?" You will give life as you are directed and guided by the Holy Spirit. He may direct you go give a smile to someone or to say a word to someone, and that one word could be the very word someone who is on the verge of suicide needs to hear. God has the ability to change someone's life just because you were obedient. You sat down and wrote that song that He has been bugging you to write for years, and you finally did it. God loves all people, and He knows what it will take to change someone's life. Because you were obedient, that life was saved. This is from my heart to yours.

If you haven't made Jesus Christ the Lord of your life, now is the time. Your new life is waiting to begin. Take His hand and live.

Father God, I believe that Jesus is Your only begotten Son. I believe that He gave His life for me. He paid the penalty of sin for me so that I may live. Lord Jesus, come into my heart and be the Savior of my life. It's Yours. I

Mary-Linda Steed

now belong to You. Father God, I thank You. In Jesus' name, I consider it done. Amen.

This will be your New Birth Day

On _____ the new me was born again.

Signature _____

Whatever follows "I am" will come looking for me. Now you make your personal list for yourself and say them out loud every day. I heard Joel Osteen and Oprah Winfrey say this on her show.

- I am blessed.
- I am beautiful.
- I am a masterpiece.
- I am creative, and my creative juices are flowing.
- I am prosperous.
- I am never broke.
- I am anointed.
- I am very likeable.
- I am wealthy.
- I am rich.
- I am a great wife.
- I am a great mother.
- I am a great grandmother.
- I am blessed at everything I set my hands to do.

Hey! Let's Celebrate You. Who, Me? Yes, You

- I am highly favored by God.
- I am loved greatly by God.
- I have more than enough money to meet every needs.
- Thank You, Lord, for the gully-washer blessing that is en route to me now so that I can be a blessing to my family and others.
- Thank You, Lord, that my physical body is healthy and whole.
- Thank You, Lord, for supernatural increase in my finances and debts supernaturally cancelled.
- Everything is working for my good because God is in control of my life.
- I am walking in my purpose.
- I am energized.
- I am inspiring others.
- I am refreshing to everyone I meet.
- I am secure.
- I am talented.
- I am valuable.
- I am influential.
- I am worthy of the best of everything.
- I am a money magnet.
- I am friendly and have lots of friends.
- I am drawing close the best people God intended for my life.
- I am sensitive to God's Spirit.
- I am a best-selling author.

- I am destined for greatness because God is taking my life and doing something with it.
- I am a world traveler traveling all over the world and helping people.
- I am out of debt, and I have more than enough money.
- I believe in myself because God believed in me first.
- I am encouraged. I am an encourager.
- I am powerful, full of the power of God.
- I am a winner.

Acknowledgments from the Words and Books of those who influenced me

Gloria Copeland

Joyce Meyer

Kenneth Copeland

Pastors Ray and Tracey Barnard

The Bible (KJV)

Bill Winston

Kenneth Hagin

Pastors Harold and Alyce Benjamin

Joel Osteen

Oprah Winfrey

CPSIA information can be obtained at www.ICGtesting.com
Printed in the USA
BVOW05s0332280514

354600BV00001B/42/P